MOOR POETS AND CONTEMPORARY MARKMAKERS

Unearthing **DARTMOOR**

OVERSTEPS BOOKS
ON BEHALF OF
MOOR POETS AND
CONTEMPORARY
MARKMAKERS

POETRY

Alwyn Marriage

Sue Proffitt & Avenda Burnell Walsh

Rebecca Baker, Janette Statton, Polly Delahoy & Josie Gould

Our Venture

Over two years many of us have laughed and picnicked together, been drenched by relentless rain and enjoyed many warm sunny days. We have witnessed the birth of a foal, heard countless cuckoos, met wild campers, stood silently among ancient stones, granite circles and burial cairns, walked the lengths of double and triple stone rows and followed mediaeval leats (human-hewn water courses running along land contours).

We have traced Bronze Age reave field systems on Holne Moor that demarcate some of the earliest enclosures of farmland in Europe; we have sat within the ruins of a 13th century farming village at the Hut Holes; we have heard about the challenges of traditional upland farming and the rewards of meadow rewilding; and we have watched many moorland birds leaving and returning.

This book shares our journey with you.

Moor Poets

Moor Poets was established twenty years ago by Pat Fleming as a community of poets based largely in South Devon, in the general vicinity of Dartmoor. It has encouraged and helped to develop in its members creative writing skills through regular workshops led by experienced writers. It has also produced four successful anthologies of Moor Poets' work, for which Dartmoor, its landscape, natural and human history, has always been a source of inspiration. The Moor Poets community has also driven independent projects with other local creative artists.

The idea for this *Unearthing Dartmoor* project grew from a successful joint exhibition in Birdwood House, Totnes, during 2019. This 2023 published book and exhibition is the culmination of two years of online collaboration, plus active excursions to chosen Dartmoor sites in a celebration of our natural environment and this creative partnership. Our website is https://moorpoets.weebly.com

Contemporary Markmakers

Contemporary Markmakers is a group of artists who have been meeting in Totnes for a very long time. A wonderful collection of very different creatives, we share a common passion for making marks.

Led throughout lockdown by Anne Pirie, who kept us together, we supported each other through very difficult times, our art triumphant where it could easily have faded. We are now knitted together, a network, still for art but fundamentally looking out for each other and jointly stretching forward.

Our group continues to be an important lifeline for us all, artistically and emotionally.

Our latest venture, *Unearthing Dartmoor*, is a joint project with the Moor Poets. Not the first time we have worked together, and not the last. Our website is https://markmakers.avenda.uk

MOOR POETS AND CONTEMPORARY MARKMAKERS
Unearthing DARTMOOR

IMAGES

Pat Fleming, Dolly Kary, Virginia Griem, Josie Gould & Alwyn Marriage

Our Exhibition

Unearthing Dartmoor represents the creative collaboration of local poets and artists working together on Dartmoor for over two years.

A large and varied body of artwork, poetry, prints and photographs chronicling and reflecting different dimensions of Dartmoor, this treasure trove of creativity was on public exhibition at the Dartmoor National Park Authority's main Visitor Centre at Princetown from Saturday 1 July to 29 September 2023. Entrance was free, offering enjoyment and inspiration to Dartmoor's locals and its many visitors alike.

Our Thanks

With many thanks in steering this project to Anne Pirie and Pat Fleming, for this book design and production to Avenda Burnell Walsh, for editorial help from Alwyn Marriage, to the publications group and to everyone who helped to make this two year project so successful.

Many thanks to Lee Bray, Dartmoor National Park's wonderful archaeologist and raconteur, who took us deep into the ancient stones of Merrivale; to Sue Goodfellow, botanist and ex-head of Conservation at the DNPA, who opened us to the botanical treasures of Emsworthy Mire; also to Norman Cowling of the Dartmoor Preservation Association who showed us around the fields and lanes of Dockwell Farm at Widecombe-in-the-Moor, where he is rewilding hay meadows, gloriously full of orchids.

We appreciate the generous grant support from both The Duchy of Cornwall and Moor Poets, and thank the Dartmoor National Park Authority for providing our exhibition venue.

Josie Gould

MOOR POETS AND CONTEMPORARY MARKMAKERS
Unearthing DARTMOOR

Alwyn Marriage

MERRIVALE

AVENDA BURNELL
WALSH
Stone rows detail
mixed media

BEVERLEY SAMLER
Stone rows
mixed media

5 pm on a sun-soaked evening
in late June which, without
summer-time adjustment means
it's 6pm, and the double row
of stones marches stubbornly
towards the sun.

Why was it necessary in Neolithic
times to determine the westerly direction?
And if it mattered so much, surely one
marker stone would have been enough
without this avenue of rocks?

The double line is wide enough to pass through
towards the setting sun. So in my imagination
I watch as figures, ceremonially clothed, or naked
and covered in coloured patterns, process slowly
through the gaps, chanting and beating drums.

And as I wonder what such a ceremony
might have meant, my mind slips forward
to a future time, when the ruin of all
we hold most dear, taxes the imagination
of races yet unborn.

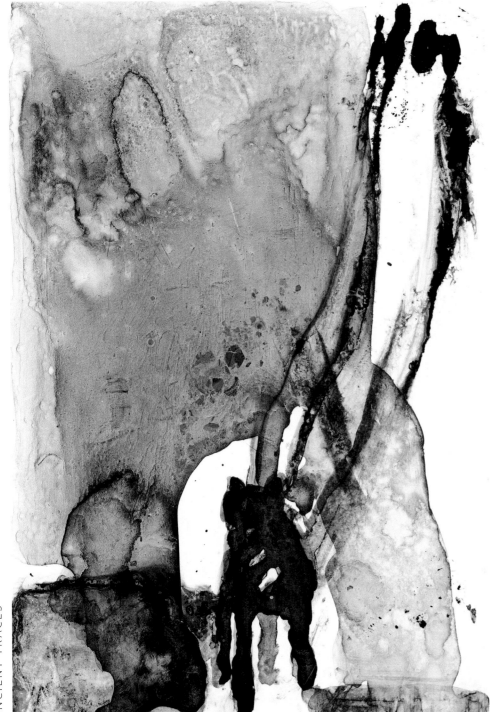

Susan Taylor

WOLF TREES

A full moon rises over Saddle Tor;
January, the moon of the wolf.
Time's passed since the wolves were here,
but many trees remember them.

On the tor top people stand,
planting themselves firm as they can
on granite. They're not rooted,
yet they're high enough
to gaze across the moon and send it
a simple human wish;

could they stay here and be wild
as the wolf trees, live long and strong
where no man, woman or wolf has left
so much as a bone on the surface.

ANNE PIRIE
*Where
no man,
woman
or wolf
& Time's
passed*
ink & ink,
collage

AVENDA
BURNELL
WALSH
*Permission
to stay*
oil

ANNE PIRIE
*Could they stay
here and be wild
& Where eyes meet
eyes III & 1*
ink and charcoal

BEVERLEY
SAMLER
Wolf trees
mixed media

Light seeps through the shutters,
slides around the wall, layer by layer
unwraps my sleep to waking
and the business of the day.
The kitchen waits for me to rearrange its shapes,
prepare the surfaces to break our fast.
It is polished by the stealing sun,
my working hands.
I knead the nourishment for body, board,
but know the smell of sweat, fleece, wool,
cold muzzles of the beasts, warm nostril breath,
pull and guzzle at the swollen teat, sweetness of milk,
straw-strewn flags and parlour's cool.

Outside, boots ring stamp of studs and leather
on the granite floor.
With pails in the clanking yard
I watch my feet on spill or chaff,
feel the texture of the morning,
rain hanging in the mist on tor and combe
that beads my lashes, hair.
Feet balance rock and marsh seep
as they feel the yield of earth for planting, gathering,
hands read its health and density.
My skin is stained with peat rust, seamed with silt.

Sometimes I feel its light, sometimes its drudgery
but held within these walls, this is the life I know,
framed by door and window, watched by moor.
There is a stillness in this patterning where I can rest;
I can revolve it steadily.

Sometimes thoughts twist off and fly up
to the high stacked rocks to find another soil, another sky.
I haven't time or space to follow them
but down here swing to the pace, the peaceful clatter
of my day's song.

Helen Boyles

A LIFE IN EMSWORTHY

ANNE PIRIE
Where eyes meet eyes II &
Sweetness of milk
ink and charcoal & ink, collage

Pat Fleming

BONES OF HOLNE
MOOR

Reading traces left in bracken, scored in stone, mounded earth,
scattered rings of rock, old fields' latticed patterns,
roundhouses, pounds, reave-walls, triple rows,
built by those who made this moorland home.

Faded paths criss-cross Holne Moor's flank,
where five thousand years ago, first land-claims
left behind hundreds of thousands of hunting years,
and Bronze Age field systems that still run for miles.

Now only broken wall stumps show us their shape,
separating tribe from tribe, human from the wild,
that once kept in their horses, cows, dogs, sheep,
kept out the fear of brown bear, grey wolves, lynx.

These empty shapes remain, lost stories of short lives,
bent thorn trees by old thresholds, hearthstones so long gone cold.
Sunken ribs of granite, weather-bleached bones,
last glimpses of these places they once called home.

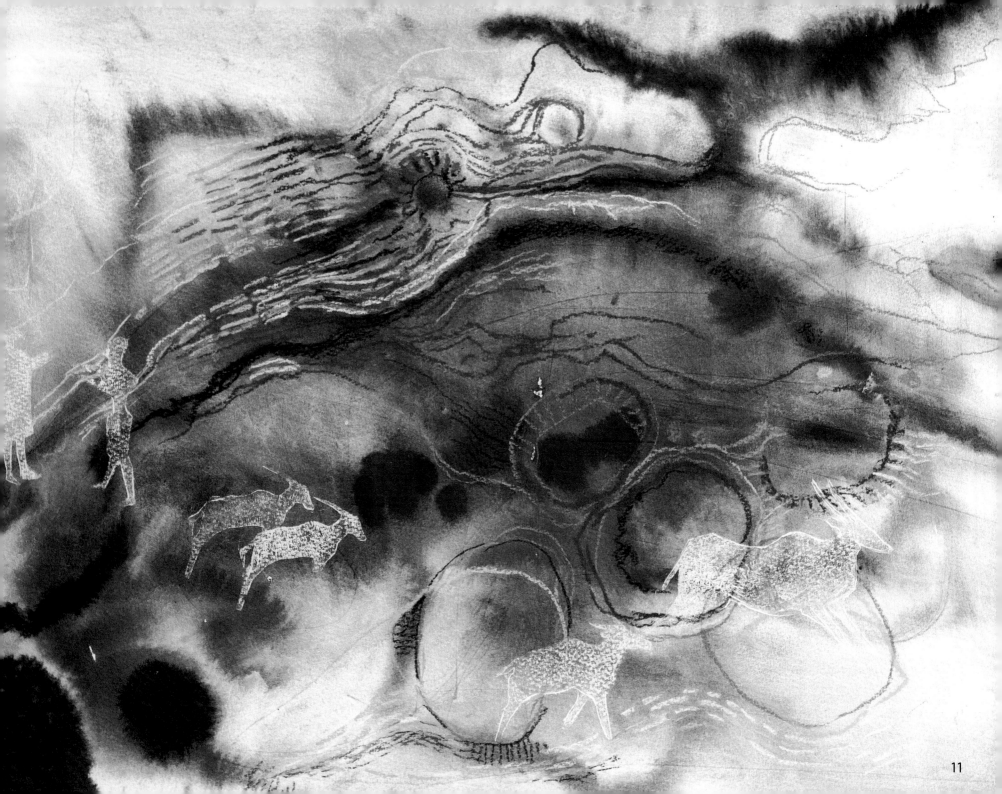

Pat Fleming

MEMORY KEEPERS

We, the stones, our long rows aligned sou'west to nor'east,
point where midsummer's sun dies back to earth
where the precious dead will leave,
where mid-winter's sun comes back to life,
where all your new-born breathe

We, the memory-keepers, keep your dead
cradled in rock rings, beneath cairns, kistvaens,
where heavy lids were once again lifted,
ancestor bones greeted by priestess song,
tenderly fingered, rearranged, returned to their peaceful beds below

At midwinter moons under mine-black skies,
you may hear our songs, high ringing voices
carried by a keening wind,
as singing your stories keeps us alive,_
singing your memories keeps us alive,
singing as we watch you, listener, pass us by.

AVENDA
BURNELL
WALSH
*What lies
beneath II*
windy field study
mixed media

13

Oh so very long ago when the lowlands were forested
and full of wolves, when there was still no word for blue,
a woman stepped out on the moor for the first time
and saw the trees were not the same as where she'd
come from, but were wind drifted, thick trunked,
trolled into faces and dancing limbs. She saw great
stones stacked as if by giants and cracked on the tors.

And what of this woman as she settled into the rhythm
of gathering and sowing, loving and birthing, raising
and dying. Did she have time for trinkets, a frill
of lichen green pinned to a bearskin cape, a necklet of
hawthorn berries to last through winter, a crown
of May blossom in spring, a glint of tin from the river
adorning the belt at her waist.

And when traders came from across the sea
with amber and gold, did she leave her fading autumn
haws on one side with sorrow, leave her lichen green
to the trees and don more lasting things.

Virginia Griem

AND WOULD SHE
STILL PICK MAY
BLOSSOM FOR
HER HAIR

BEVERLEY SAMLER
*May blossom in
her hair &
preliminary sketch*
mixed media
15

Simon Williams

LULU

Until she stood, she could have been a sheep,
her pinafore the colour of a Devon greyface fleece,
her shoes as like to hooves as you might ever see
and her eyes forever sparkling like drops of heather tea.

She can run the bog-grass like any moorland ewe,
hopping clump to clump, as field crickets do,
but none, the turning buzzard nor the shy cuckoo
can giggle to the gurgle of the brook like bright Lulu.

I saw her in the bottom field, I'm sure that it was she,
but as I tried to reach her, she skipped behind a tree.
When I got there, all I found was soggy moor and me
and a stonechat, a fast jack hare, a jet black bumblebee.

ANNE PIRIE
Until she stood:
another soil,
another sky &
Until she stood:
on the edge of
light &
Until she stood:
life beside the
mire
ink, collage

Simon Williams

OVERNIGHT

I met her in the doorway
as she hurried me inside.
On such a Dartmoor night as this,
I wasn't going to ride.

Sitting by her glowing fire.
sipping at her broth,
the firelight drew me to her,
like a lantern draws a moth.

As we sat, she told me
of her life beside the mire,
the snows and storms, the sun at dawn,
the blossom on the briar.

All night we slept in wooden beds,
both boxed and curtained round.
I listened for her breathing,
but I never heard a sound.

At morning, when I left,
I asked her for her name.
She said her mother called her Lulu
and I could do the same.

She'd gone back in before I knew
I'd left my hat inside.
When I went in, the rooms were bare
the roof blown tempest wide.

ANNE PIRIE
Until she stood:
life beside the
mire (detail)
ink, collage

BEVERLEY SAMLER
Emsworthy
mixed media

ANNE PIRIE
All her life
ink and charcoal

Simon Williams

HERBALIST

BEVERLEY SAMLER
Darkling sky
print

JOSIE GOULD
Moor mystique
oil on panel

Walking quickly across the mire,
I thought I knew the route,
but algae on a boulder
got the better of my boot.

My ankle was a twisted mess
and swollen to the bone.
I couldn't walk, I sat and called,
but I was quite alone.

Then, as the sun slid down the tor
a woman came to me,
all shawls and lace, a kindly face
but older than the hawthorn tree.

She pulled plants from her basket
and water from the brook.
She fashioned a cold poultice
and bound it to my foot.

She stayed with me and as we talked
I learned she lived nearby,
that she had been here all her life
beneath this darkling sky.

I must have slept, as it was dawn,
my ankle quite restored,
I walked up past a ruined farm
to the high road 'cross the moor.

When I told my tale of aid
much later, in The Prince,
a farmer said 'That's old Lulu,
been dead a decade since'.

BEVERLEY SAMLER
Location sketch
charcoal

LOU REED-DAUNTER
Moor ponies
markmaker photography

Close your eyes.
     Fingers in ears.
Breathe in deeply through your nose.

Smell the fear
under the dusty, musky scent
of unbrushed, rough haired
horse flesh
     wild from the moor.

Unplug your ears.
Listen to the whinnying
snorting, unshod hooves
on hard tramped sand.

Open your eyes to
the jostling and shying
the whites of their eyes
flashing as they skitter
     try to hide

the lad in the pen
showing off the paces
of mares and foals
poking
small stallions with his crop.

Notice the hard eyed woman
calculating how much.

Rosie Barrett
BYSTANDER AT THE PONY DRIFT

Pat Fleming

MERRIVALE GLIMPSES

AVENDA BURNELL WALSH
Roads cross Dartmoor 1 & 2
mixed media

The moorland farmer on his ATV shouts
driving a creamy wave of bleating ewes
east towards Foggintor
black-white dogs keeping them tidy

I herded all my sheep from the back of my chestnut cob, who I trusted with my life.

two long woolly lines unwind like yarn
He stops, calls the three collies
come bye, come bye
telling them to flank out,
keep the flock off the busy Princetown road
metallic clanking of his trailer
cuts through skylark song
until the bleating fades

Shatter
chilled
trammeled by January wind
Bark crumbles like biscuit into
my hand.

Downy Birch seeds

Like a sweep of skylarks!

Susanne Conway
ESCAPE

don't want to go home so I head to the old tramway,
the granite rocks, the tor my son thinks looks like an orca.
A cyclist rises over the claw of the hill, out of the mist, so sure
on those pedals. I used to be like that. Now it's enough to walk
in drizzle and drifting fog through icy water, past sheep scat,
only the ground as compass: three rocks and a path on the left.
Remember that for the way back.

At the gate, pull the bolt across, snap it shut. Here to choose:
turn and keep walking, brushing through thorns, into the hills,
or go to those you love. The crane winch squats
by the glassy water. I want to curl up beside gorse, heather,
their blinding yellow and bruised purple buds.
Be like them, unfurl, begin again.

JULIA FINZEL
Bench tor
markmaker photography

PAT FLEMING
Like a sweep of skylarks
field trip notes

Standing at the bottom of our Dartmoor garden
beside the compost heap, cutting muddy roots
from fresh-tugged leeks, relishing each sharp slice.

Upriver, above the oaks, a young buzzard mewls,
urgent alarm-calls splintering the evening's peace.
I carry on at the wormy pile, adding leaves to paper,
horse-shit, weeds, old veg,
all treasure to feed tired beds.
From nowhere, cool air swishes down,
the young wide-winged buzzard swoops low, heading home.

At this same moment, five hundred miles north,
COP 26 opens to address this fragmenting world,
where heads of state call each other out,
making promises to be broken, forgotten.

I would be there, I wanted to be there, to make sure
my alarm cries were heard by someone, anyone, maybe no-one?
At least, like young buzzard, giving everything to my yowl.
But I didn't get on that train, or sleep on the floor of my friends,
or stand in a windy wet Glasgow street handing leaflets
dressed as a turtle, sun-bear or pangolin,
indeed anything needing its voice to be heard.

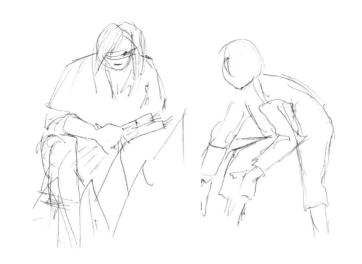

Instead, here I am, slicing white leeks,
delighting in their perfection,
how anyone would love them just steamed – so sweet!

I stop, listening to the radio's Pacific voices,
as Palau's President reprimands us sharply
  "You might as well bomb our islands."

Women of Samoa, Vanuatu, Fiji speak passionately
  "We have no hill to run to."
    "We are not drowning, we are fighting!"

I wave my knife in solidarity, so angry at our species' stupefied thrall,
turned away from our legacy, shunning upcoming generations,
whose soil and sea and air we hold in the smallest of actions.

So many of us mewling deep down like young buzzards
for safe return to a home place, somewhere solid
to rest and renew, somewhere to perch and remain
as certainty recedes on an outgoing tide.

Pat Fleming
FIGHTING, NOT
DROWNING
14/11/2021

JOSIE GOULD
*Light breaks on
the water, stop*
oil

BEVERLEY SAMLER
Field sketch
mixed media

29

Hello, old guy! Who are you
and what brings you out here
to sit for hours on the moor?

Is this your blanket? Was it
cold last night? How long
have you been here?

I almost walked straight past you,
would have done, if you hadn't
suddenly risen from the grass

and taken off across the moor
without a backward glance,
fading into sheep-grey mist.

Your dark exterior belies
a heart that's full of music.
Look, look,

the fragments of last year's
dried and broken grass
fly up, transformed,

and undefeated by
the wind and rain,
take wing – and sing.

Alwyn Marriage
ROUGH SLEEPER

RACHAEL BENNETT
*Dartmoor
markings no 8*
Indian ink and pigment

ANNE PIRIE
They held its light
ink

These great boulders were built into walls for a purpose.
They were planted here for a four-square scheme;
by a man and a woman who planned to make good
on land that many would say was not worth the effort,
and, yet, this couple found method to thrive here.

They built themselves a life among willow and bluebells.
These boulders remember a whole tribe of children
running around the newly-walled meadows,
their springtime delight at the birth of foals,
gentle, magnificent, by their dams' sides.

These boulders remember the mother rocking the cradle
and singing the song of new life's arrival.
These boulders remember the maid, milking the cow
for the house; her singing the sweet, sad anthems
of where was love, when would it happen for her?

Everyone sang in the evenings. They sang by rush light
and firelight, together, with only their faces illumined.
By and by, it was only the singing that held
the farmstead together, for mire crept towards them,
and mire was no friend to a family of farmers.

Year by year, it closed over the lower pastures;
the fine water meadows all turned to morass.
There wasn't the hay for a run of harsh winters,
and no neighbour had any to spare.
Winter came, at last, with the starvation of cattle.

Leaving a farm for a lack of livelihood,
leaving a farm for a lack of love;
it all boils down to the same kind of sorrow.
These boulders may have been here before anything,
anything much had happened at all,

but they still hold, somewhere, within their hard hearts,
the grief of the people they sheltered for lifetimes.
They still hold the grief of the day the dream died,
and the people of granite and song had to leave,
to take up more or less ordinary lives.

Susan Taylor
CONJECTURE OF AN EX-FARMER
AT EMSWORTHY MIRE

JANE ELLIS
Majestic Dart boulders
mixed media

BEVERLEY SAMLER
Sketch
ink

We all helped build the chapel, so take pride
in the way it snuggles in the valley near
the clear life-giving waters of the leat.

Although most days, between our lips
teeth grip the comfort of tobacco pipes,
never would we smoke inside the chapel

so before we enter on a Sunday afternoon,
we carefully knock the ash out on the gatepost
then leave our pipes to shelter in the wall

tucked between granite slabs to await
our exodus, while we raise gruff voices
in familiar hymns of praise.

But the days we welcome visiting preachers
are the best, when The Old Rugged Cross
rings out in Ernie's deep rich baritone

to float out through the door and up the hill
as it has always done since the day he discovered
music and his father taught him the words.

And for a while pipes, preachers, farming tasks
and rough Dartmoor weather are all forgotten
as Ernie opens a window into heaven.

Alwyn Marriage
PEAT COTT PIPES AND MUSIC

BEVERLEY SAMLER
Merrivale II
mixed media

AVENDA BURNELL WALSH
Tucked between granite slabs
oil
35

HUMAN TOUCH

36

Here they sleep, Methodist and Quaker
each in their earth beds in this quiet space,
watched by guiding texts of duty, piety.
They lie beside the river that had fed their lives
from where it rose and tumbled from the hills
into a harnessed rush and clatter on the mill wheel
powering their labour in the beating forge.
Here they ground and hammered to its deeper roar;
now they rest,
looped in its lapse and shine.

An old print holds the memory of that community
before the emptying of World War I,
each man proudly furnished with the weapons of his trade
and with the faith that grounded them.
And this had spilt from high hills in the voices
of evangelists from rock pulpits
echoing a call that drove the heart and muscle
to another service raised in stone chapels
ringing to another song.

Now the fabric of their structures crumbles;
stealthily reclaimed by Ivy and by Clematis
buried stories struggle up towards the light.
In their garden Quaker, Methodist, sleep on by the river,
washed and renewed by its travelling,
held in a waiting by their headstone messages.
And each year villagers climb to the rock
where Wesley preached, repaint it white,
while down below restoring hands and voices
work to open up the paths and signs that guide us
to their histories.

Helen Boyles

FINCH'S FOUNDRY, STICKLEPATH

AVENDA BURNELL WALSH
Industry
ink

RACHAEL BENNETT
Dartmoor markings no 1
Indian ink and pigment

Alwyn Marriage

The path forked from the well-worn track
through overhanging bushes, turning
left to wind more steeply up the hill.

I soon discovered it's better not to be
encumbered by a bag. Even if it isn't heavy
it tends to swing, to throw off-balance.

From time to time we doubted this
could be the right way, or that we
would ever reach our destination

but when we arrived, just below the brow,
there was no mistaking the white rock,
balanced above the almost sheer drop

we had scrambled up. We paused,
turned round to be rewarded by a clear
long view back down along the valley.

Was it like this for those men and women
who followed the preacher to this isolated
spot, leaving their normal life, to be assured

that it was worth the effort, that baggage could
be left behind, that it was possible to take a longer
view, assess what, on reflection, might be worth

listening to, working for; how it was that
words, flowing for an hour could so soon
inspire the hearers to a better life?

AVENDA BURNELL WALSH
The path forked
oil

JOSIE GOULD
Midsummer moor
mixed media

M ire, marsh, the words open a wet space,
plash, squash in the mesh of consonants.
They sound the need for wellingtons,
protective wet gear,
for the careful placing of feet.
From the margins we skim eyes on a surface
twitching, flickering with life and light,
watch out for a quivering, that bright green
that might suck us in.

Instead we graze eyes from safe edges
on the glance and whirr of wings
above the stems and flower heads,
blue shards hovering on cuckoo-flower's white,
see in the mind's eye deeper down
weed ribbon, sprays of leaves
float and spread in that clear space
to sift and drift of nutrients
unbroken by our clumsy spill and stumble,
holding their own balancing.

Helen Boyles

EMSWORTHY MARSH

JOSIE GOULD
Emsworthy mire 1 & 3
ink

Rebecca Gethin

Waters run just below the earth
scattered with yellow stars of tormentil.
A river's birthing is like a fledgling's lift.

In places, you hear grumbling or chanting
and maybe sometimes laughter
until when you search through the reeds

you're bewildered to find a rill trippling
over stones among ragged robin,
bog myrtle and water forget-me-not.

And though the syllables may change
water never forgets it's a safe nest here
to well from the dark ova of springs.

LOU REED-
DAUNTER
*Mire water 7, 6,
8 & 9*
markmaker photography

MIRE
42

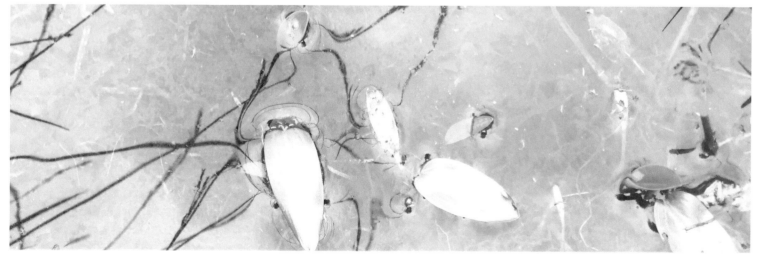

Sue Proffitt

EMSWORTHY MIRE

JOSIE GOULD
Field work & River Dart
crayons & watercolour

1 Water
Let's talk about water.
Sunlight catching shining skin
that divides and re-forms
through each interruption –
water murmuring to itself,
throaty, gurgling, soil
holding water then letting it go
to run over its body
like a child that won't be stilled.

2 Board-Walk
Archipelago of broken stems,
coppery leaves, mud blossoming
into islands floating motionless,
and between them the black plunge
down. I could wade in now,
pull up the world heavy and wet
in my hands,
run my fingers over its light crust
feel the ache in my arms grow
as the core pulls me, leaden and lightless.
To survive the weight of the world
you must spin on its skin
like a water boatman.

3 Rain
This is where rain sleeps,
dreams, held without boundaries,
only porosity. Only the soak of soil,
drinking until each capillary,
each worm-hole, brims and bubbles,
the open throat of earth filled
with what can't be swallowed.

4 Spongy moss
Around my pressed-in finger
soil sucks, hungry as a calf,
but these aren't lips, warm, waiting
for what comes next – spit,
a kiss – instead, innumerable
tiny leaves sink under my finger
then rise up again as if the press
of my flesh hadn't happened,
as if I'm no more than a breath
blowing on their radiant green faces.

5 Heron
lifts up, slowly flaps away.
There must be fish.

6 Light
Imperative, like blood.
Here it is, trapped amongst reeds
and sparking. Here, light runs,
shimmering. Half-close your eyes
to see the separation of things
disappear. Look at one blade of grass, half-
submerged – there, at its base, a wink.

7 Water
will not be stopped.
My body listens.
Remembers.

Helen Scadding

We walk in circles,
bewitched by fields of blue
in a land that can't stay still.
It bubbles up.
Its rocks grow fur.

We step uncertainly
skirting the sinking places
preparing for the pull
held back only
by the cuckoo's call.

The black water
winks with charms
lit by stars of moss
and the flickering
of white wings.

RACHAEL BENNETT
Humps
markmaker photography

ANNE PIRIE
Black water
ink, collage

ANNE PIRIE
A lesson in vulnerability
ink

JOSIE GOULD
Mire 2
mixed media

Helen Scadding

GRANNY MIRE

Y ou soak it all up -
  our small confessions, meanderings,
accidental spillages.

Our young heels dance on your lap,
soft as dough.
Your old paths keep us safe,
enfolding us, season by season,
until we reach out beyond them,
then you gently pull us back
and we lay ourselves down
beside you.

We are merry   the chattering stones
of Merrivale   see how we lean towards
each other or lean away to study
the horizon we can never cross

listen on the night of a gibbous moon
when the skies are clear   you might
hear us whispering   right gossips we are
tellers of tales   keepers of the lore

Virginia Griem

Helen Boyles

MARKMAKERS

AVENDA BURNELL WALSH
Molten granite
watercolour

JULIA FINZEL
Farm near Widecombe
markmaker photography

Stones, stacked or solitary,
are the bones of our histories
breaking the swell of land
as we wade through, reminding us
of something deeper than we see.
We can try to reassemble
their scatterings,
read the anatomy of origins
where we hauled ourselves up
from earth to light,
raised homes, defined ourselves
through boundaries, forged tools
to delve and cultivate,
carved our initials everywhere.

In rain and sunlight stripped and washed
of time's accretions,
we see them glint and heave
their elemental script,
see the bones of our stories
in their first shine
when ground was yielding
and winds soft.

And when the climate turned
a keener blade
to unpeel our securities
we looked down, looked up
for other gifts to dig and raise,
spoke in the shapes of stones.

Across the knotted sea of heath
a granite cross, one-armed,
tilted westward,
stamps its stubborn silhouette
on space, dials its slow shadow
round the base beneath a wheeling sky,
the soaring lark.
Drilled by rain and sun, greened
by the patient calligraphy
of vegetable growth
but forged in fire and ice,
its blind face
outgazes distances,
is crushed with the glitter of quartz,
the tears and sweat of our endeavours
crystallised.

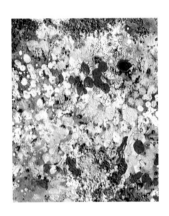

Simon Williams

THE TROUBLE WITH
TRYING TO SKETCH
STONES

RACHAEL BENNETT
*Granite no 3,
no 2 & no 1*
mixed media

S tones stay always
just not the way they're drawn.
Stones are complexity,
with their compatriots – moss
and lichen – fitting to the pits,
the pocks, making their
green dew upon it all.

Stones know we don't have time,
can't spend centuries catching
their landscapes, the aeons
they've devoted to allowing
wind, water and things that gnaw.
A few scrawled lines won't
make a start at them, startle them.

Stones aren't even troubled
by our names for them;
'Granite' has a certain ring,
hard like tors and ridges.
'Stone' is such a simple sound,
feels imposed, the way we've made
walls outside, fire indoors, soup.

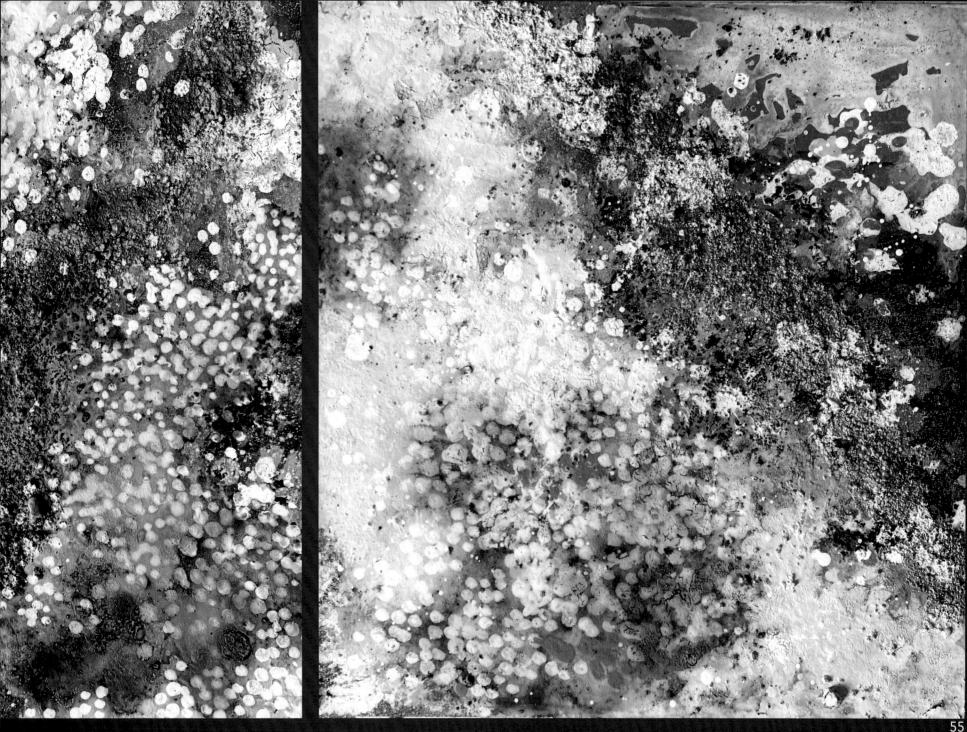

Tom Woodman

Tom Woodman

WHAT LIES BENEATH

woke up soiled,
 smeared through the moss,
 lapping up cow shit and piss.

 Sucked on sheep bones,
 gorged myself on silt,
filling my guts with last year's leaves.

 Slid fat under the bridge,
 licked oily past the docks,
 savouring the sewage pipe.

 Gaping my dirty mouth,
 to puke into the sea.

Never mind the fossil record, the real deal is in the cavities and abscesses where the corpses used to be. Just below the skin-deep, leeching, unfounded and undone. Rinsing their teeth in the drinking water, filtering it through their ribs.

Biology and geology symbiose their moves in 4/4 million time, to shape a palimpsest landscape.

A fossil-to-be subsides into the mire, bloated, diminished.

Granite is everywhere and always, boils through the tops, simmers and seethes under the gorse and in the bogs.

Faded tattoos and scars on the skin of the moor. Contours strangling the summits.

Wind and rain have scraped and scoured away everything that wasn't moor and tor, leaving only what is yet to be sculpted. The landscape holds the negative space of what used to be.

The artist paints the lichen and the lichen paints the rock. The gorse drags my legs and the blood paints my skin.

AVENDA BURNELL WALSH
Sucking at bones &
Meeting neanderthal
oil

Sue Proffitt

EAST DART

She flips her hips slip-slide
over stones' cold shoulders
nudges over, under,

gathers her lace tatters,
eddies, pools,
spins on herself

runs away
gathers herself up
again, tumbles

into places
where rocks mouth secrets
beneath her brown skin,

sometimes she catches
herself in a thought,
dark, poke-worthy,

something to circle
and probe,
spirals an answer

gallops downstream,
face dark as whiskey,
face distilled light,

shimmies in her white,
flicks glitter at air,
races ahead

of herself as branches
thud and knock against her
like hearts

chuckles and chucks
the stones' faces,
then suddenly slows

in the wide-skied place
opening eye to eye –
a mirror snagged in twigs.

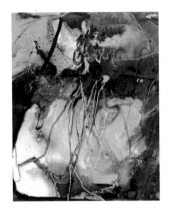

Virginia Griem

JANE ELLIS
*Pockets of
space I & II*
mixed media

The White Wood is throttled
with bracken and bramble,
its lush pillows of long stemmed
moss buried in a smothering of new
undergrowth. Only the path is clear
of this invasion with its sandy bed,
its fringe of hewn granite.

It follows the pipe, which is thick
as my body, funnelling water to
Paignton – water destined for seaside
taps, to be lost in the washing of dishes,
the flushing of toilets. The path pulses
to its constant flow, gravitates to the
town which has no great river of its own.

The drought's hit hard, and the Reservoir
itself barely seems to hold enough for such
a task. Its' level is mud-low, reveals a
drowned bridge where a clever engineer
once leant from his horse, decided
– *here I'll drown a valley, build a reservoir,*
lay a pipe thick as my body,
all the way to Paignton.

Helen Boyles

PEAT

Anatomies are grooved on sheets of rock,
crushed by the weight and shift
of time's deposits
or emerge intact to startle us.
Our lives are swaddled there deep down
beneath our feet, crumbled
to peat's slow thickening.
Breath exhaled by plants, by us
across millennia
is held there in its dark sleep.

We can slice, stack, heave it up
to heat our homes.
But it dries slowly, burns its pages
steadily, softly sifts and shrivels
to bleached ash.
Holes left in the ground
gape wounds in memory.

In the layers of the dreaming mind
we visit it, return to origins.
Water-fed, it swells with our stories,
the shed leaves and rains of seasons,
enfolds the print of foot and hoof,
cycles our leavings, our passages,
to new purposes.

It can consume, exhume;
sometimes, suddenly, by spade cut,
throw to sight
the blind face of a sleeping ancestor.

JANE ELLIS
The ancestors
dance
Chinese ink

BEVERLEY SAMLER
Field sketch
mixed media

RACHAEL BENNETT
Natural art no 3 & no 1
mixed media

Alwyn Marriage

This dark grey block of rock
is patterned with lighter patches

I wonder about the ancient artist
doodling such decoration, surmise

that lichen, or even grass,
grew up here not so long ago

clinging fast to its firm
foundation for a while

but wind and rain, the beat of hooves,
the searing summer sun

have wiped away all evidence of growth,
leaving only light grey maps into the past.

Rebecca Gethin

LIKE A VISITATION

Waxcaps well out of the sward
like corals erupted from ground
– luminous, fleshy and shining.

Their colours rejoice in themselves.
Underground their anatomy
is a mass of hyphae and mycelia

bonding with soil particles
to nourish their fruits with lipids,
elements and enzymes

that flow from the centre
and along invisible conduits.
So much we can't know –

if we delve around in the core
we destroy microscopic connections
that keep everything going.

JANE ELLIS
Symbioses II, I
& glimpses
mixed media

You hear them first
 piu-piuu piu-piuu
look up in the sky
see nothing but blue

piu-piuu
   a silver fish-flash
comes twinkling toward you,

a shoal
like a shawl
unravelling stitch by stitch
down the sky
till one turns,
another follows
and they all climb,
speckling the blue,
vanishing head-on into light.

They bring us our winter,

Rebecca Gethin

GOLDEN PLOVERS
ARE COMING

Helen Boyles

WHITE WOOD

JULIA FINZEL
beside Bench Tor
markmaker photography

Since the carving of the Moor these pale-skinned oaks
have hugged the valley sides
around the river's flux and shine.
They sift and gather light to stipple bark, the woodland floor,
measuring the seasons, sun, where falling years
are layered in moss, tree boles and limbs
stealthily tapestried.
They are rooted in earth memory, sunk
in a fungal web exchanging nutrients
that nourishes and lattices community.
They draw on buried sources
to sustain themselves, in slow time
twist their own shapes to the pull and fall of sap
in their spreading and decline.

We feel we know them, may have entered them
in dreams or captured them in myth.
And they know us, cycle their histories and ours
across millennia.
They have shaded hunts and foraging,
have filtered heat, supplied our hearths and heart wood.
Here, now, they muffle underneath the forest track
evolving technologies, the pulsing monologue
of water poured and stored in concrete
in the flooded valley bed, turned and sluiced
through metal, pushed and channelled
from down deeper far beyond this ancient nursery
to serve distant towns and purposes,
keep us afloat.

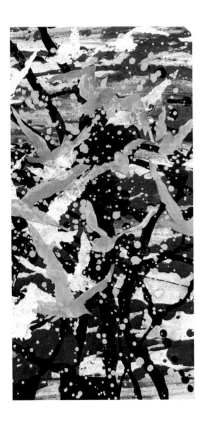

Alwyn Marriage

RACHAEL BENNETT
*Moorland birds &
preliminary work*
acrylic & collage

s it rough at sea?
    I doubt it, there's
    no wind to speak of
    and the sun is warm.
Are they following the plough?
    No, it isn't harvest time
    and anyway,
    this land belongs to sheep
    and ponies, never could
    grow an arable crop.

All of which explains my surprise
    that I can see
    flocks of gulls
all flying up this river valley
scattering an untidy trail
of plaintive mewing.

Last night the calls of cuckoos
echoed from the woods
reminding me it's spring –
the time of growth and pairing
when the romance of this nomad bird
overcomes distaste for no-mad
life-destroying piracy.

A couple of kilometres up the hill
the sound of tumbling water
almost, but not quite, obliterates
the two-note mocking call.

stand
on a rock   six foot square

feel
like a statue   something to study

watch
a stonechat   top of a gorse bush

tolerate
constant surveillance of cuckoo song

study
water   flow elaborate lace of reed threads
tump

admire
lichen's motley
clothing for granite

believe
fern fists
shudder a little
before breaking
tender
upright

queen bumble bee
dark as molasses
dances
patterning air
with wing burr

be caught
in her way of hypnosis

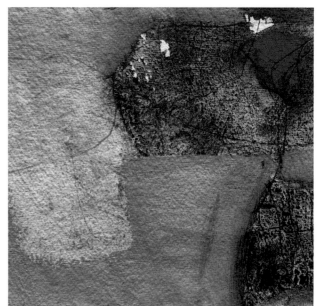

Susan Taylor
BEE COURT AT
EMSWORTHY MIRE

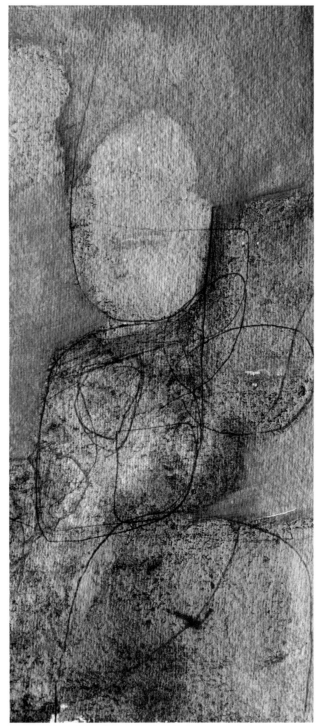

JANE ELLIS
Looking deep,
Granite building
blocks I & II
mixed media & ink on
khaki paper

Rebecca Gethin

MOSS

At the feet of the trees
there's an underforest
tiny conifers and palms
       fern fronds
green star clusters
       tufts of baby hair

so small they're only named
       in Latin
rhytidiadelphus, dicranum, thuidium
you need a lens
       to tell them apart

all their parts are named
       calyptra, seta, sporophyte
as leaf shapes are named
plicate, complanate, papillose

they live on rain
       reproduce in rain
       and rain lives in them
they live without words
but words make them live for us
like spells or prayers.

Helen Boyles

TRYING TO CAPTURE
EMSWORTHY
CUCKOOS

W e follow the plump echo
bouncing and rebounding across space
its teasing source eluding us,
near at hand one moment
then half-muffled floating off.
The singer loops his flight
through camouflage, barred breast
leaved in shadow, yellow eye
a gleam of pale fruit in the boughs.

We hunt him across open green,
a scattering of hawthorn scrub,
through gaps in stone walls
from one meadow to the next.
Artists, poets, squint and strive in images
and words to catch the fading in and out
of voice and shape.

He 'singeth as he flies', apparently,
but throws no arrow up against the blue.
Instead he lures us out across the spongy ground,
slide of mossed rock, welling brook,
tosses back his challenge and recedes
now here, now there behind us from the trees
beside the red-roofed barn.

Clambering the rise and plashy scoops
we stumble on to hear him ring his mocking monody
invisible around a crouched form fixing camera sights
on far and middle distance from a low scrape,
waiting through the long day for that trophy shot
the bird withholds and guards
along with the secret of his partner's hidden nest
and her deceiving strategy.

JOSIE GOULD
*Red roof barn
& detail*
oil on panel

T ormentil,
undeterred
by high moor's
inhospitality
studs the cracks
with flashes of
startling yellow.
Potentilla,
doubly powerful
as herbal remedy
and as fragile beacon,
chilled and down-trodden
yet surviving the worst
excesses of the weather.

Alwyn Marriage

ONE AND THE SAME

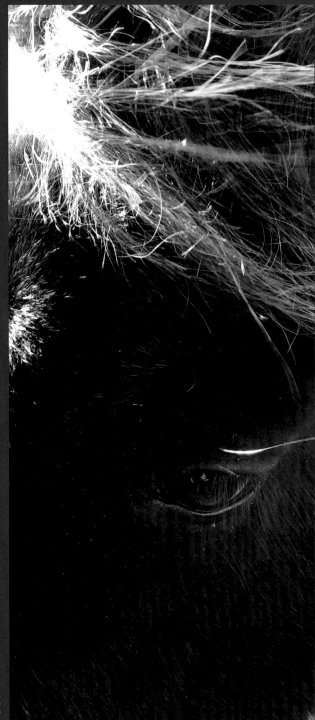

Legs that were tightly folded for
eleven months, still don't quite work
in sync, so have a tendency to wobble.

The mare's instinct is to lick the newborn
clean, though it seems she hasn't learned
what to do with her trailing placenta

while the foal, who is now experiencing
the first sharp pangs of hunger,
has yet to discover where to find milk;

and on this wild, cold moorland
there must be at least a hint of regret
for the warm security of the womb

in the same way that we can feel homesickness
for something we've forgotten or never known
as we wobble our way through life.

On spring-greened turf
new foal, just-dropped,
struggles up, birth-dazed
from first spill
to splay-legged sway.

Rest, then staggering
a long-legged dance
to nourishment,
learning to plant feet,
hold itself together,
push down and up
through stumble
and recovery,
secure a place.

Milk-scenting, seeking muzzle
nudges flank.
Numbed by labour,
trailing the pink glisten
of the afterbirth,
too spent to help,
the old mare waits,
eyes fixed on nothing,
statue-still
but shading helplessness.

There is patience,
There is time.
The day wheels slow.

For now, the clouds are soft,
nearby, the shelter of a barn.

Life will clamber up from sleeping,
stretch out through protecting shade,
sway, dazed in the light a while

then answer to a beckoning
from close or farther off –
through shifting seasons,
sometimes unsteadily
but stubbornly,
will make its way.

LOU REED-
DAUNTER
Ponies 1 & 3
markmaker
photograpy

Alwyn Marriage
HIRAETH;
DARTMOOR BIRTH

Helen Boyles
EMSWORTHY FOAL

N o cuckoo. No bluebells.
Just a newborn foal.
We know it's newborn, as its mother
still has the afterbirth dangling.
We know it's newborn as it still
has a wobble in its drinking straw legs.
We know it's newborn as it makes
sounds that aren't quite horse, yet.
The other ponies, known for their
prehensile lips, make attempts
to debag the picnics in my carrier.
No cuckoo. No bluebells,
just birth and search for sustenance.

Now you're a month,
you own the moor,
cheeky as a stoat.

Happy to nuzzle,
take a stroke of neck,
magpie confident.

When we walk on,
you pony up behind,
try to eat us, coats first.

At the gap
in the farm wall,
you finally give up,

trot back to the mare,
grazing up slope,
waiting like a Madonna.

LOU REED-
DAUNTER
Ponies 4
markmaker photograpy

JULIA FINZEL
White Wood
pen and ink sketch

Simon Williams

EMSWORTHY FRESH

Simon Williams

SECOND MEETING

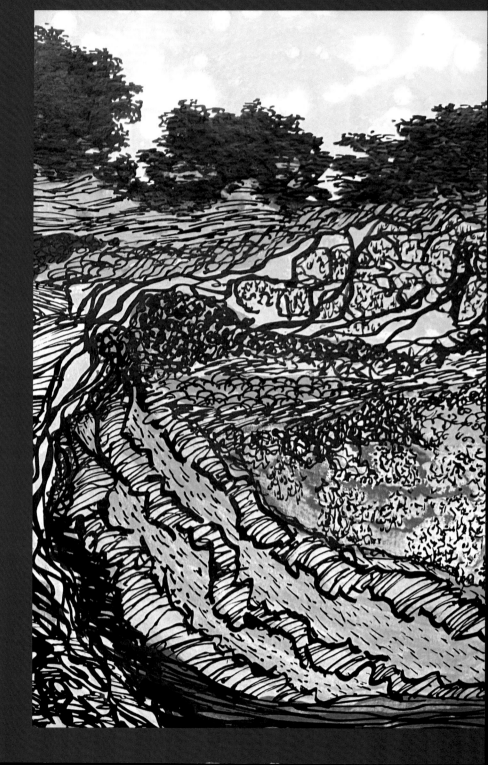

There's a leap in the heart of things,
precious, precipitous, poetic.
Consciousness rises
from out of the depth of sleep,
like a brown trout
out of the womb of wild water.

What is the nature of the lure,
the attention which flickers into attraction
and, seemingly, towards life?
If the line tugs,
where will the thread lead?

It is so very gentle,
the creep of the light,
but it doesn't take long
for the blackbird, the wren,
the thrush, the robin
and all of the rest to join the throng.
They have plenty of songs to spare
and a rhythm as sweet as the blossom.

May buds become musky scented,
as bees shake them free.
Light dances on branches in petal.
Here, time is liquid
and dreams are all for renewal.

Susan Taylor

AS THE MAY BUDS

RACHAEL BENNETT
*Dartmoor markings
no 9 & no 6
fragment*
Indian ink and pigment

At first there's only a scattering
on the bumpy grass by the gate.

I pick my way among rocks
seeing the wash of mauve
grow denser in the distance

grass beaded with mire-damp
sheep reaching for food among stems
bent with the purplish weight.

I stop to count cuckoo calls.
How many voices?
A bird nearly always unseen.

Along the chunky wall –
stones as settled as those
the landscape has thrown up –

flower heads turn the grass
into a sea that will soon recede.

None have planted themselves
in the water of the mire.

Susan Jordan

EMSWORTHY
BLUEBELLS

JANE ELLIS
Immersed
collage & Chinese ink

RACHAEL BENNETT
Sketchbook fragments
mixed media

AVENDA BURNELL WALSH
Wild flowers
watercolour

Make a model with papier-mâché, plaster-of-paris, clay.
Lay out the moor with every tor in the correct proportion
to its height, each leat and river valley. Write the name of
everything you know: villages, stone circles, reaves, old mines.
Don't forget the stepping stones, the holy wells, the crosses,
and don't forget the car parks. Mark Visitor Centres and public
toilets. Use foil to show the reservoirs or paint them blue.
Mark the drovers' roads, monks' trails, tinners' paths.

Virginia Griem
MAQUETTE

Turn your model over. Did you make it hollow, so you
can show the unearthing, the tin lodes, the mine shafts?
How deep in the ground water bubbles and sucks until
it streams and rivers out – you must add that somehow –
and the buried railways, tunnels, pipes, pumps.

Don't forget the morning light as it comes racing out of
the sea, the sudden mist coming down, the rain
rushing in from the west, hoar frost on winter bracken.
Paste on the raven, the cuckoo, the whinchat, wild ponies
with their suckling foals, and everywhere the greyfaced sheep.

Last you must add the watching. Only you know
how it feels and how well it fits.

AVENDA
BURNELL WALSH
A slice through
mixed media on board

JANE BEATRICE
Stone circles
pencil field sketch

Graham Burchell

QUIET GREEN FIREWORKS
ON JULY 4

GRAHAM, POET AND ARTIST,
WAS A CENTRAL FIGURE WITHIN
MOOR POETS, WHO HAD HOPED
TO JOIN US ON THIS PROJECT
BUT SADLY DIED RIGHT AT ITS
BEGINNING. 'COTTAGE PI' IS HIS
LAST PUBLISHED COLLECTION OF
POEMS

Here is shadow's corner of damp cleave,
downstrokes worn by water for water:
unruly tilts and drops. Gravity insists.

Here is shadow's corner of break, shift and timeless gouge,
seized by a bitter salad of flaring sedges, ferns, roots
and small insurgencies of holly.

Here is shadow's corner, never powder dry,
not even after cloudless days late June into July.
Here is a humus factory belching breath of moss and leaf.

Here is shadow's corner mulched with beech and holly husks.
And there is a bed of stones for skimming across the Dart;
an armpit of the river, gentled, foam-freckled,
a lady-in-waiting.

ANNE PIRIE
*Roots
and small
insurgencies
& Skimming
across the
Dart*
flashe and wax

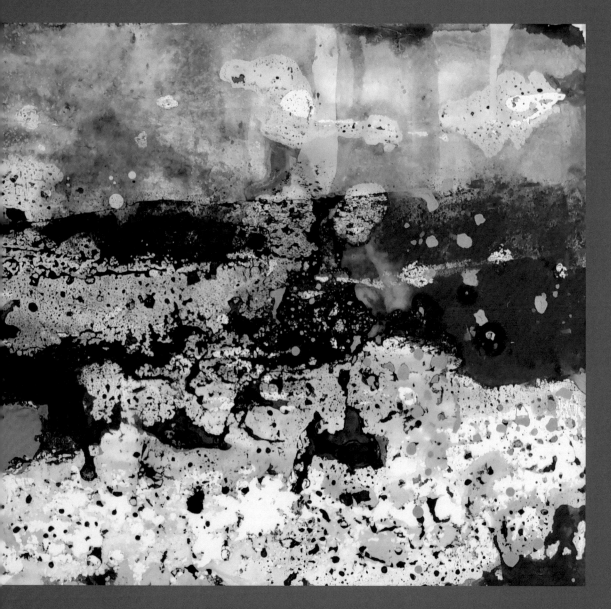

Pat Fleming

YOU ALMOST MADE IT

t was almost a full moon,
when you almost made it to the moor.
Instead, we, a triad of poets carried you up.

Sprays of tormentil lit the path
on our climb to Bench Tor.
You'd have loved these crannies:
wild amethyst thyme clinging to rocks
damp ferns, your green fireworks,
laced with rain
dark overhangs beneath sheer cliffs
strewn remnants of ravens' nests.

We took you in our hearts and packs,
as your 'Cottage Pi' poems came along.
Leaning into White Wood's mossy slabs
we invited each other to feast on your words
reading to each other
drizzle running down our necks.
The twisting oaks leant in,
listened too.

W ho might bring it to me
this scrap of land, abandoned
by tinner and tiller, mine-scarred,
stone-drawn, bracken-strangled
and bog-bound.

Who might bring me its prickle
of gorse, a miner's pack of bread
and meat with a prayer for fine
weather to last him a week as he
walks out to the Wheal Emma Leat.

Who might bring me a stone bladed
plough to seed a furrow within the reave.
Ask only the tellers of fireside stories for
here on the moor there are no angels.

Here on the moor there are no angels.
Why would there be on these heights with
not a church in sight. Those beneath the
hills do not on the whole offer the sort of
worship that welcomes angels to their liturgy.

Nor is there a single unicorn among
the moorland ponies. These are bred
the sturdy kind, unlikely to lay a head
in a maiden's lap. Here the only cloven
hoof belongs to a sheep – or the devil.

Listen at dusk on a foggy evening, you could
well hear the Wisht Hounds calling.
You would be wise not to follow them or
let yourself be pixie-led through the mist.

JANE ELLIS
*Abandoned
tin mines*
mixed media

ANNE PIRI
*Who are we,
listening*
ink

Virginia Griem

HOLNE MOOR,
CORONET

4 INTERLOCKING
POEMS

Let yourself be pixie led through the mist
along the leat which flows upstream
as if by magic, through the dried out
gorse scorched by Spring drought, on
to the hulk of Bench Tor.

In this light it is a stack of bronze shields
laid careless on the moor by a giant,
his battle done, his sword redundant,
his only wish to sit and watch the
ravens' sky dance.

Search for footprints, they are set
in the stones, as if he paused and stood
and looked about and thought to himself
if I were to build a castle...

Virginia Griem

HOLNE MOOR,
CORONET

4 INTERLOCKING
POEMS CONTINUED

f I were to build a castle
I would build it here, on the High Moor.
I would build it of glass, carpet each room
with emerald moss and blood red sedum,
find me a hollow stone big enough to bathe in,
sleep on a mattress of lady's bedstraw,
pillowed in may blossom.

I would dine at a granite table
fit for a lion, sit on a great throne above
the trees where a leat would flow down stairs
in a cascade of pools full of pebbles bright as
jewels. At night I would watch the sky for
a falling star, ask the owl and nightjar
who might bring it to me.

JOSIE GOULD
Glorious autumn
oil on panel

AVENDA BURNELL
WALSH
Stone rows
mixed media

97

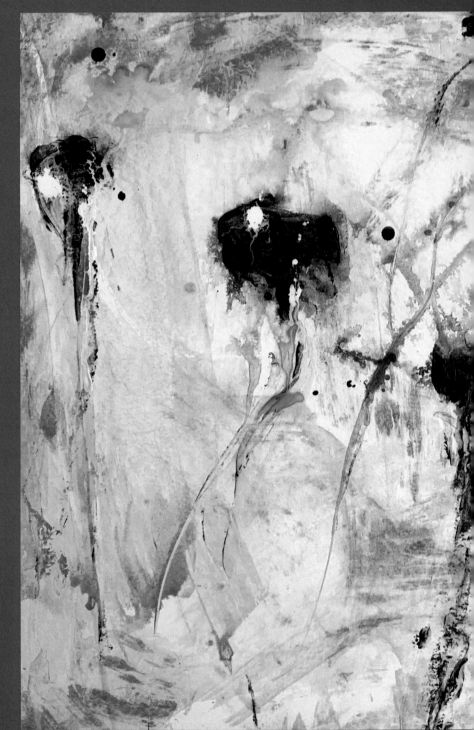

n an almost June, which feels like almost April
  at Emsworthy Mire, bluebells appear, small as pixies,
and we hear the first call of the cuckoo.

How can it be the first call of the cuckoo,
expected, for certain, before the almost of May?
Its chiming is charming over the ruinous farmhouse
and the enigmatically painted roof of the barn;
a blue and red image straight from tourist calendars.

This is the month of true glamour here:
poets, photographers, painters; markmakers all,
come to hear the morning birdsong,
not only the pirate bird's hullabaloo,
but, also, the innocents tending their nests.

We come to breathe the moss's breath.
We come to dwell on crystal sky.
We come for the whisper of sycamore.

Susan Taylor
ON YOUR MARKS

AVENDA BURNELL
WALSH
Moor whispers
acrylic

ANNE PIRIE
*Held back only by
the cuckoo's call*
ink, graphite

99

Alwyn Marriage

EARTH SCULPTURE

AVENDA BURNELL
WALSH
*Unyielding
granite*
mixed media

ANITA REYNOLDS
Foggintor
field sketches &
concertina book

To build
castles, bridges, sky-scrapers
or even modest homes
we add material – brick,
stone or metal – which
we've taken from
elsewhere.

Earth has a different method:
to create majestic tors
or those gigantic faces
our minds impose on
vast protuberances
gazing over the landscape
or out to sea.

Each time it rains, a little more
soil slithers off, rubble shifts
and slips over shifting centuries.
What was always temporary
wears away, to reveal –
like the sculptor perceiving
the perfect form within the stone –
these strange, unyielding
granite giants of the landscape.

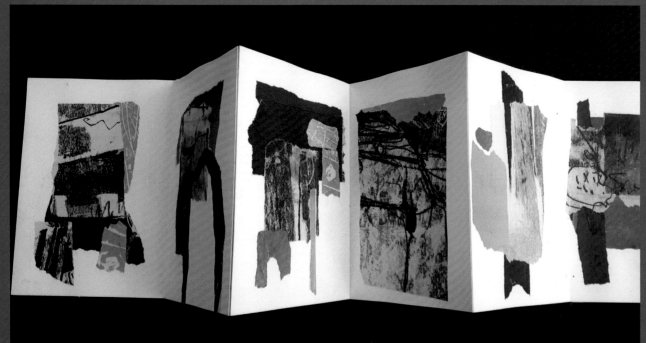

B one caves, stone coffins,
granite walls worn down by time.

Mine workings long disused.

Things needed for the life to come
smirched with peat and long-settled earth.

Roots of plants severed above ground
or perished in harsh wind.

Spent breath of digging animals.

Insect body-cases, flesh of worms,
snail shells, crisped spiders.

Cobweb lattices of spent thought.
Grief that never saw the light.

AVENDA
BURNELL
WALSH
Unearthed
ink and oil

JANE ELLIS
Dusk
mixed media

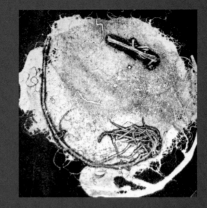

Anita Reynolds

FOGGINTOR QUARRY
& TRACES OF
FLORA, FAUNA
AND MAN

W hen distant views are obscured by mist you have no choice but to notice the things beneath your feet, your world becomes the small area of ground that surrounds you. It was such a day when I made these small prints. I walked methodically up and down, 50 paces in each direction to form a gridded area and collected items that interested me. I printed them, cleaned the items and scattered them back onto the moor, the litter items I took away.

Human traces are now so evident and irreversible that we have given a name to this new geological time, The Anthropocene. I pondered on the futility of picking up a small amount of waste materials from a very minute area of Devon, a mere speck on our Earth. I concluded that every act however small is a step in the right direction, and that we all have our part to play.

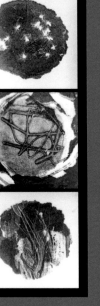

ANITA REYNOLDS

*Foggintor Quarry &
Traces of Flora,
Fauna and Man &
detail*

collage field study & monoprints
(10×10cm) made on location
using water washable ink and a
gelatine plate

SILVER BIRCH BARK	BRACKEN	GRASS SEED
OAK BARK	BRISTLE BENT	MAT GRASS
MOSS & LICHEN	SHEEP FESCUE ROOT BALL	GRASS & SOIL

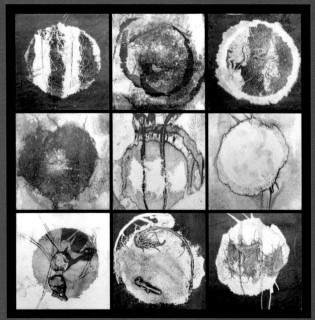

HORSE HAIR & GRASS	WOOL & MAT GRASS	WOOL & MAT GRASS
WOOL & HORSE HAIR	COW DUNG & HAIR	WOOL
WOOL	HORSE HAIR & DUNG	COW HAIR & DUNG

METAL WASHER	RUBBER BAND & COTTON THREAD	CAR RADIATOR
CLIMBERS CHALK	WATER TANK LID	TIN FOIL
HEXAMIN ARMY STOVE	CAMPERVAN CURTAIN RAIL	CIGARETTE BUTTS

through the old oak beside our gate
come songs from between-time

sitting on the shin of a longstone, fallen
near Merrivale's great standing stone

time stretches out, becomes generous
unsullied by the torrid world

I will not tell. The truth is rooted in my silences

a fallen goat willow across the Venn Brook
a hundred hopeful seedlings jostle for light

above Holne Chase woods, a full moon
is eaten by the clouds
becomes a dragon's eye
slides down the dragon's back
vanishes into a cloud pool

listen – the wind's keening carrying ancestral clinks of knapping flint
ragged stone into fleet arrow heads, spear points razor sharp stone
knives good for flecing, flensing, carving, keeping

poetry is like the blood from stones
where crimson words ooze into song

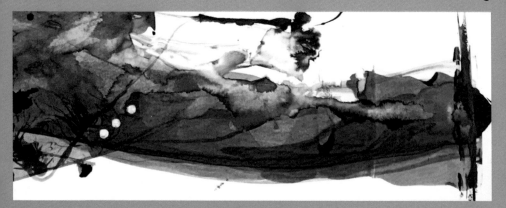

*Working words
and sketched
images*

FRAGMENTS FROM:

JANE BEATRICE, ANNE PIRIE,
BEVERLEY SAMLER, JANE ELLIS,
JOSIE GOULD, JULIA FINZEL,
RACHAEL BENNETT, ROSIE
BARRETT, ALWYN MARRIAGE,
PAT FLEMING & AVENDA
BURNELL WALSH

FRAGMENTS

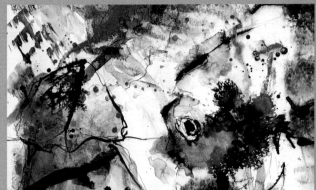

rivulets of rain drizzle slowly down through thick
moss carpets
wrapping trunks of twisted oaks

the armoured fearsome blackthorn, my mother
... of sphagnum and bog mosses, lichens
Micellular fungi, cotton and purple moor grass

shards of unfinished stories hang around withered
homesteads

moor grounded weather – rubbed

this land belongs to sheep and ponies

up here, where there is more air than we can easily breathe

... all shall return,
And we are one is written
Under my eyelids,
In neon

we walked together,
a trinity,
to see the deep wooded oak tree
moss-mouldy,
and smell the mushroomy ferny place

... a purified Dartmoor,
had taken our breath away,
and frozen our fingers

... time to go home,
leave the granite stone,
wrap ourselves in orange blankets
and eat raspberry cake

last night's storm becomes the river's roiling
seething and writhing, liquid amber boiling

a sister of the mosses and fungi
Mites and worms,
Daughter of the gorse and bog grass

... this is my family, here are my beloveds

out on the moor, contemplating freedom

gorse scratching, gouging, mark making our thighs

and yet, when the world is falling apart, short-sighted humans who've forgotten our place,
even your own blood pounds, thrumming along

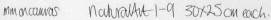

mm on canvas   Natural Art 1-9 30 x 25 cm each.

and scrabbled long through thick and thin, rough
and tougher, sticky and prickly, tender lichens pale
and magic, heathers
new and shouting colour, embryonic spruce trees
fledging their tiny
beginnings

and marks escaped us
but we found one or two and caged them in our
notebooks

111

Glued together by walking boots, workshops and zoom

Our wonderful group, makers of marks and word strings. During the two years of location work, zoom meetings, workshops and general brainstorming we have made lasting friendships. Artists have honed a new love of words, poets have become fascinated by charcoal, wax and paint. We have all grown. You will find our names throughout the pages.

The Contemporary Markmakers who travelled the journey with us, both by zoom and by walking boot, are Anne Pirie, Beverley Samler, Rachael Bennett, Jane Ellis, Josie Gould, Jane Beatrice, Avenda Burnell Walsh, Julia Finzel, Lou Reed-Daunter, Susan Miller, Sue Kellam, Anita Reynolds, Dolly Kary, Rebecca Baker, Jo Gibson and Maggie-Anne Smith.

The participating Moor Poets are Alwyn Marriage, Helen Boyles, Helen Scadding, Pat Fleming, Rebecca Gethin, Rosie Barrett, Simon Williams, Sue Proffitt, Susan Jordan, Susan Taylor, Suzanne Conway, Tom Woodman and Virginia Griem.

Rebecca Baker, Suzanne Conway, Virginia Griem, Pat Fleming & Josie Gould at Bench Tor

Lee Bray, Stuart Miller, Virginia Griem, Susan Miller, Beverley & Keith Samler at Merrivale

Anne Pirie & Dolly Kary

Fragments

The Fragments pages will take you with us on our journey, our adventures, fleeting phrases and marks captured as we worked together, in small groups and large outings, side by side in all weathers and sharing workshops more virtual. This section is a tribute to the work as it emerged. It is by all of us. For you. Perchance to tempt you in.

You might walk our paths, find strings of words, sketch small ideas, run your hands through the wild flora and photo some fauna. We hope you do. Take some paper and a pencil. Breathe in some Dartmoor. Unearth a bit for yourself.

Farmer Norman Cowling, Rachael Bennett, Richard Boyles with Pip & Suzanne Gray-Conway at Dockwell Farm

Hugh Marriage, Lee Bray, Richard and Helen Boyles, Pip & Alwyn Marriage at Merrivale

Julia Finzel & Dolly Kary

Dockwell Farm with Suzanne and Claude Gray-Conway, Rick Jenkins, Pat Fleming, Helen and Richard Boyles, Pip, Norman Cowling, Rachael Bennett & Beverley Samler

Above Emsworthy with Susan Taylor, ecologist Sue Goodfellow, Rebecca Baker, Maggie-Anne Smith, Anne Pirie & Simon Williams

Dartmoor unearthed

Dartmoor granite rose up, molten, from the depths of the earth over 300 million years ago, and ancient humans shaped the landscape here from Mesolithic times, 10,000 BC. Woven through these pages you will see these old rocks red, hot, bubbling, cooled then finally worn down. Unearthed for you.

Prehistoric human traces date back to the late Neolithic, some 6,000 years ago, and Dartmoor has the largest concentration of Bronze Age remains in the United Kingdom, making it one of the finest archaeological landscapes in Europe. The climate was warmer when our settler ancestors began clearing the forests for homesteads, cultivation and for livestock grazing. That is why you will read ... *On the tor top people stand, planting themselves firm as they can on granite. They're not rooted, yet they're high enough to gaze across the moon and send it a simple human wish, could they stay here and be wild as the wolf trees ...*

In these pages that history is re-imagined by poets and artists.

When you come to Dartmoor you will find your own magic, unearth the stones for yourself. Bring your boots. And wear clothes for changeable weather.

Jane Ellis on a rock

Avenda Burnell Walsh & Beverley Samler battling the Merrivale wind

Bev, cleaning up after tumbling into the ancient tomb in search of her windblown art materials

Josie Gould making marks

A catalogue record of this book is available from the British Library
ISBN 978-1-906856-95-3

Copyright: individual artworks and poems by the named artists and poets.
Copyright of the book: Oversteps Books Ltd
For permission to use any of the book's contents, please contact the Managing
Editor of Oversteps Books: alwynmarriage@overstepsbooks.com

Images by Contemporary Markmakers
Poetry by selected Moor Poets
Design and layout by Avenda Burnell Walsh
Photographs by the group
https//:markmakers.avenda.uk

Published in the UK by Oversteps Books Ltd
www.overstepsbooks.com
Printed by Imprint Digital, Devon

book
oversteps